D1478263

IMAGES
of America

ABERDEEN
PROVING GROUND

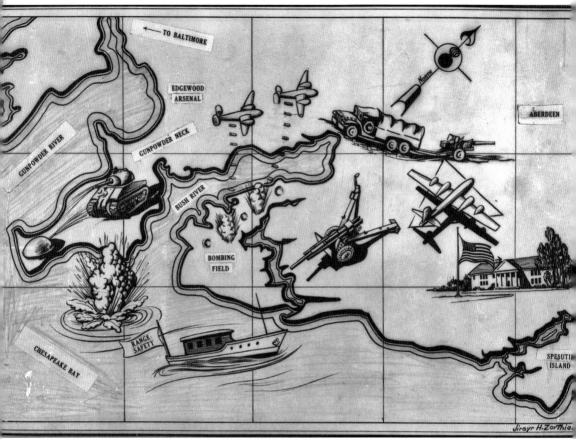

MAP OF ABERDEEN PROVING GROUND. This stylized map, a drawing from the World War II era, shows the general military activities on base and where they take place. The map is a good reminder that about half of the more than 70,000 acres covered by the base is water: areas of the Gunpowder and Bush Rivers and extending out into the Chesapeake Bay. (Courtesy U.S. Army.)

ON THE COVER: "TOONERVILLE TROLLEY." Aberdeen Proving Ground had over 40 miles of railroad track, some of which is still visible today. Three gauges, or different widths, of track carried trains that hauled everything from passengers between the gates and work areas to the heaviest of materials and weapons. The passenger train seen here was called the "Toonerville Trolley" after a newspaper cartoon of the time. (Courtesy the Historical Society of Harford County.)

IMAGES
of America

ABERDEEN
PROVING GROUND

Bill Bates
with a foreword by
Maj. Gen. John C. Doesburg (Retired)
Former Installation Commander, APG

ARCADIA
PUBLISHING

Published by Arcadia Publishing
Charleston SC, Chicago IL, Portsmouth NH, San Francisco CA

Printed in the United States of America

Library of Congress Catalog Card Number: 2006940480

For all general information contact Arcadia Publishing at:
Telephone 843-853-2070
Fax 843-853-0044
E-mail sales@arcadiapublishing.com
For customer service and orders:
Toll-Free 1-888-313-2665

Visit us on the Internet at www.arcadiapublishing.com

This book is dedicated to those who have paid some personal price on behalf of their country: the citizens of Harford County who, in 1917 and 1918, gave up their land and livelihoods for the creation of Aberdeen Proving Ground; the more than 100,000 military personnel who have trained or worked at APG; the citizens who have supported the military in their roles as employees, contractors, and volunteers; the officers and policy makers who have sought to balance mission and concern for the community; the soldiers and civilians who sacrificed their health or their lives during the production and testing of ordnance and chemicals; and those soldiers and civilians who, from World War I to the present, have gone "over there" to serve the cause of freedom.

CONTENTS

Acknowledgments   6

Foreword   7

Introduction   8

1.   From Sandy Hook to Harford County   9

2.   Chemical War: World War I   31

3.   The Readiness Is All: Between the Wars   49

4.   A Town of 30,000   73

5.   Soldiers and Citizens Together: World War II   81

6.   A Legacy of Innovation   113

ACKNOWLEDGMENTS

Aberdeen Proving Ground garrison commander Col. John T. Wright has been an enthusiastic supporter of this project from the beginning. Colonel Wright enlisted the help of Maj. Gen. John Doesburg to write an appropriate foreword for the book in honor of the 90th anniversary of the establishment of Aberdeen Proving Ground. My thanks to both Colonel Wright and Major General Doesburg for their responsiveness and example of leadership.

My point person for this project was Jeffery K. Smart, command historian, Historical Research and Response Team, U.S. Army Research, Development and Engineering Command, Aberdeen Proving Ground (APG), Maryland. Jeff was Virgil to my Dante, my personal guide to seeing APG through his historian's eyes. Whatever is accurate in this book is there because of Jeff's guidance; whatever is in error is due to my inattention. Thanks to Jeff and his staff, especially William H. Hauver, program support assistant.

My appreciation also goes to Peter Kindsvatter, Ph.D., staff historian, U.S. Army Ordnance Center and School; Randy Davis, military historical collections analyst for LGB and Associates, contracting at the U.S. Army Ordnance Museum; and to Tim Tidwell, exhibits specialist, U.S. Army Ordnance Museum, for his gift of CDs of scanned photographs.

Thanks to installation historian Mark Gallihue for his insights into APG's history.

For sharing their postcard collections, thanks to Jim Bleier, Marlene Herculson, Terry Noye, Nancy Sheetz, Bill Walsh, and Ed Ward.

I thank everyone who has supported me with their best wishes and their enthusiasm for the book—the list of your names would fill this book.

Thanks also to Richard Sherrill for introducing me to the APG materials; to David Craig for his support of Harford history; to Jim Chrismer for making history "click" for my daughter; and to the Harford County Chamber of Commerce Military Affairs Committee, led by Linda Walls and Rick Weiner.

Thanks to Maryanna Skowronski for continuing our fruitful relationship on behalf of the Historical Society of Harford County; to the entire team at Arcadia Publishing, especially my editor, Lauren Bobier; to my wife, Mary Ellen, for her gift of time during the writing of this, my fifth book for Arcadia; to my daughter, Emily, for finding some perspective in my musings on history; and to my son, William Geoffrey, as he joins the U.S. Marine Reserves, following the example of service given to him by his marine grandfather, my father-in-law, the late Eric Smith Ruark, who fought on Iwo Jima.

FOREWORD

Founded at the outset of the United States involvement in World War I, Aberdeen Proving Ground has experienced many changes over the last nine decades. The history of the installation is a colorful quilt and includes the histories of the former Gunpowder Military Reservation, Fort Hoyle, Edgewood Arsenal, Ordnance Training Center, and Camp Rodman. Since 1971, they are collectively known as Aberdeen Proving Ground, comprising over 76,000 acres of land and water in the environmentally sensitive Upper Chesapeake Bay region. Soldier training, breakthroughs at the leading edge of science, and the development of battlefield-dominating weapons systems have been a major part of Aberdeen Proving Ground's history. Today Aberdeen Proving Ground's primary missions are still in support of the national defense: training of Ordnance Corps personnel; research and development of new materials and chemical and biological defense; acquisition of major warfighting, detection, and protection systems; and research, development, acquisition, test, and evaluation (RDAT&E) of all types of military equipment and systems in support of the Armed Forces of today and tomorrow.

Needless to say, over its 90 years of service to the nation, Aberdeen Proving Ground has evolved to keep pace with modern training, technologies, and warfare. The area is poised to experience the greatest change in mission and personnel since World War II as a result of the Department of Defense 2005 Base Realignment and Closure actions. The installation that has been the "Home of Ordnance" since its inception will send the Ordnance Corps training mission to Fort Lee, Virginia, just as it saw the departure of the Chemical Corps training mission starting in 1979 when the Chemical School was reestablished at Fort McClellan, Alabama. Over the next several years, the RDAT&E mission will expand to include communications and electronics systems. Now is an appropriate time to reflect upon the enduring contributions of the men and women who served at Aberdeen Proving Ground over the last 90 years and to welcome the newest members of the Aberdeen Proving Ground family.

—Maj. Gen. John C. Doesburg (Retired)
Former Installation Commander, Aberdeen Proving Ground

INTRODUCTION

In 1917, just before the U.S. involvement in World War I, the Ordnance Command at Fort Hancock was outgrowing its proving ground at Sandy Hook, New Jersey. The army needed to develop and test weapons and ammunition, or ordnance, of increasing power. It also needed to research the chemical weapons being used in Europe. Sandy Hook's closeness to New York Harbor meant the proving ground activities would have to be moved elsewhere.

Col. Colden Ruggles, the commanding officer at Sandy Hook, first tried to relocate his Ordnance Command to Kent Island, on the Eastern Shore of Maryland, but was rebuffed by the outspoken farmers and citizens who were concerned for their land and livelihoods. However, an old friend of Ruggles, Edward Stockham, suggested looking at Harford County. Stockham showed the colonel land between the Gunpowder and Bush Rivers and the vast farms and fields that supplied Aberdeen canneries with tons of tomatoes, the sweet local delicacy shoepeg corn, and peaches from Poole's Island.

The area was distant from major cities but connected to them by an excellent infrastructure of railroads that supported the canneries. The natural separation between the Aberdeen and Edgewood areas of the grounds was good for keeping the chemical production and testing away from the ordnance areas. And the amount of land exceeded what Ruggles had been looking at on Kent Island. Ruggles offered the families and farmers of Michaelsville fair compensation to leave their land and told business owners in Aberdeen and Edgewood that they would be compensated for lost business. Some 30 years and a series of court and congressional battles later, a handful of those business owners received a fraction of what they were promised.

During the fierce winter of 1917 and 1918, Ruggles moved the Ordnance Command to what was first called Edgewood Reservation and built some semblance of regimentation upon the frozen fields. The post officially opened on December 14, 1917, and the first gun was fired on a snowy January 2, 1918.

ABOUT THIS BOOK

My goals in writing this book were twofold. First, I wanted to provide an introduction to Aberdeen Proving Ground (APG) for those who have never been past the gates. And second, I hoped to bring back memories for those who served or worked on the base and for their families. If you have memories to share, or corrections to suggest, I welcome your comments. Please contact me at bill@harfordbooks.com. For more APG history, visit www.harfordbooks.com.

One

SANDY HOOK TO
HARFORD COUNTY

LOCOMOTIVE. Sandy Hook Proving Ground in New Jersey was the "Home of Ordnance" before the Ordnance Command relocated to Harford County in Maryland. This train was the predecessor to APG's "Toonerville Trolley," pictured on the cover of this book. This first chapter shows where the Ordnance Command came from, why it relocated to Harford County, and what the area was like before the army bought the land. (Courtesy U.S. Army.)

SANDY HOOK PROVING GROUND. Sandy Hook Proving Ground had been a part of operations at Fort Hancock since the fort was established in 1898, along with the Engineers Corps and the Signal Corps. In the background, passing ships safely ply the waters leading to New York Harbor. (Courtesy U.S. Army.)

FORT HANCOCK. The entrance to Fort Hancock shows what a formidable structure protected New York Harbor. Any ship passing by was in range of its batteries of cannons and mortars. The latest in a line of forts that guarded New York Harbor since the War of 1812, Fort Hancock remained active from 1898 until its deactivation on December 31, 1974. It is now operated as part of the National Park Service. (Courtesy U.S. Army.)

FORT HANCOCK, INTERIOR FORTIFICATIONS. Atop the fortified walls, soldiers drill as they load the big guns for firing. Thanks to the developments at the proving ground, Fort Hancock boasted a number of batteries with guns ranging in size from 6-inch to 12-inch caliber to respond quickly and accurately to everything from large vessels to small, fast torpedo boats. (Courtesy U.S. Army.)

CONCRETE GUN BATTERY. Over the years, a series of forts and guns at Sandy Hook protected New York Harbor. Each iteration of defenses was based on the best technology available. For example, the army began a granite masonry fort in 1859 that was obsolete before it was completed due to the development of rifled artillery, which could blast brick and granite walls to dust. Concrete came to the rescue. (Courtesy U.S. Army.)

CONCRETE GUN BATTERY. Concrete, a new material, was used to build two gun batteries on Sandy Hook in 1895—one of the two is seen on the previous page. A new fort was needed to house the soldiers who would tend the battery. In October 1895, the army began plans for Fort Hancock at Sandy Hook. The fortified walls, as seen here, gave better protection to the guns and soldiers. (Courtesy U.S. Army.)

CONCRETE GUN BATTERY. The original battery guns were equipped with hydraulics to raise and lower them for protection. Too costly and unwieldy for quick reloading, the system was replaced with counterbalanced guns that rose quickly when a weight attached to two balancing arms on the gun was dropped and then sank back into position from the gun's recoil. (Courtesy U.S. Army.)

METAL GUNBOAT, FORT HANCOCK. This small gunboat is a reminder that metal was once an experimental material for making war on the open seas. While there was no documentation with this photograph, perhaps the boat dates from an earlier period than the fort itself. (Courtesy U.S. Army.)

U.S. LIFE-SAVING SERVICE STATION NO. 1 AT SANDY HOOK. Begun in 1849 in response to the number of shipwrecks off the Jersey coast, the service was a series of 40 stations every 10 miles from Sandy Hook to Cape May. In 1915, after a series of nationwide expansions and reorganizations, the Life-Saving Service joined the U.S. Revenue Cutter Service to become the U.S. Coast Guard. (Courtesy U.S. Army.)

U.S. LIFE-SAVING SERVICE STATION. Service as a lifeguard was a serious occupation. This small structure at Sandy Hook served as home for months of duty. In addition to constant vigilance and responding to sailors in danger and shipwrecks, the lifeguards underwent daily drills much as the army servicemen did. The result was a team that relied on each other and that knew every inch of beach and water. (Courtesy U.S. Army.)

DINING ROOM, QUARTERS ONE, FORT HANCOCK. The stately dining room in Colonel Ruggles's home, or Quarters One, is decorated and the table set for a festive occasion, possibly a holiday dinner. (Courtesy U.S. Army.)

DINING ROOM, QUARTERS ONE, FORT HANCOCK. The same room seen from another angle shows the ordnance symbol in the stained-glass windows on either side of the room. A military-themed frieze enhances the decorative mantel to the far right of the room. (Courtesy U.S. Army.)

MESS HALL, FORT HANCOCK. Simple stools and sturdy tables emphasize the spare quality of life for the regular soldier, although the tin ceiling adds a touch of elegance. Here, as always, the purpose of mess was to load the men with energy for the often backbreaking work of the common soldier. (Courtesy U.S. Army.)

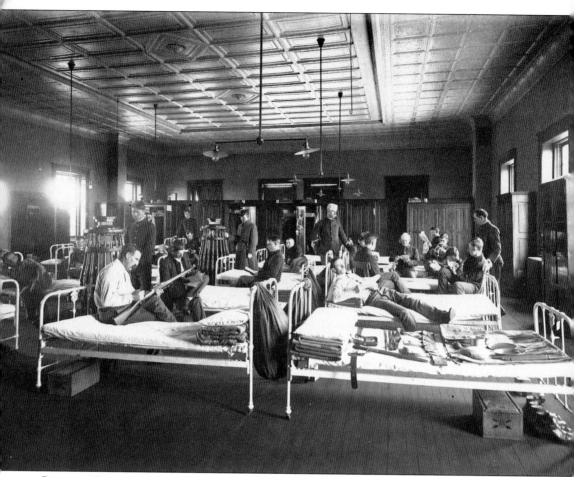

COMPANY BARRACKS, FORT HANCOCK. The enlisted men at Fort Hancock lived in four company barracks that housed 80 soldiers apiece. Residents included 1st Sgt. Tom Mix from 1901 to 1902, who would later become a cowboy movie star in the 1920s and 1930s. Here the men play cards, clean rifles, and catch up on reading. (Courtesy U.S. Army.)

SHELL FILLING, FORT HANCOCK. Part of the Ordnance Command was not only to test weapons but also to test the explosive shells and the various chemicals that filled them. In this way, more effective ammunition was developed. Sandy Hook Proving Ground afforded the space for the ordnance activities. (Courtesy U.S. Army.)

ORDNANCE TESTING, FORT HANCOCK. The Sandy Hook facility became too small for ordnance testing. Officers from the Engineers Corps and Signal Corps frequently complained of ordnance accidents and misfires that damaged offices and barracks. The order was given for Colonel Ruggles to take his Ordnance Command elsewhere. (Courtesy U.S. Army.)

BOMB TEST. This direct hit of a phosphorus shell from a biplane onto the crow's nest of a warship is a spectacular example of ordnance testing that took place during and after the war. This test took place in 1923 off the North Carolina coast, one of a number of testing locations. (Courtesy U.S. Army.)

SMOKE SCREEN TEST, NEW YORK HARBOR. Smoke screens are effective ways to keep an enemy from seeing troops, tanks, or planes. Here a plane drops a smoke screen curtain across New York Harbor in 1924. Of course, the proximity to the great city limited certain types of ordnance testing, especially when working with the new poison gasses being used by the Germans—another reason for ordnance relocation. (Courtesy U.S. Army.)

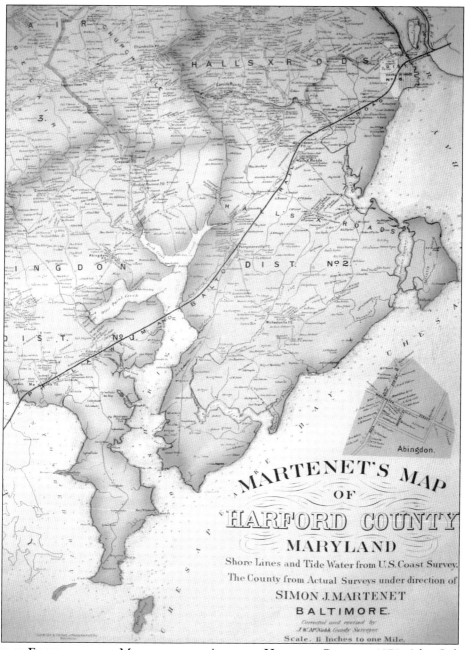

MAP OF EDGEWOOD AND MICHAELSVILLE AREAS OF HARFORD COUNTY, 1879. After Colonel Ruggles was rebuffed by Kent Islanders, he took his search for land to Harford County, specifically the areas south of the dark, diagonal line of railroad tracks. Edward Stockham, an old friend and retired officer, suggested the land to Ruggles. Stockham prospered as a cannery owner, so he had little to gain by encouraging the army to purchase the farms that supplied his business. The town of Michaelsville lies toward the center of the landmass on the right. To the far right is Spesutie Island, which was later purchased by the army. Once the deal was made, hundreds of families left their homes and farms, and all roads were fenced off by the army to prepare the area to become the new "Home of Ordnance." (Author's collection.)

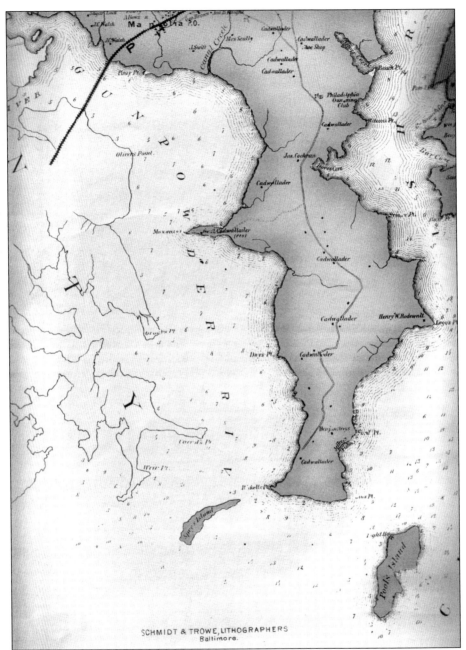

MAP OF GUNPOWDER NECK, 1879. The 1879 map is as good as any to show this area, because not much had changed over the generations since some of the first settlers in the New World founded the town of Baltimore on the Bush River. Of course, the town became known as Old Baltimore once the city on the Patapsco River grew in prominence. This map shows the names of homeowners and landowners. Poole's Island sits on the lower right of the map. Farmers there grew Poole's Island peaches. The Chesapeake area was also a haven for sport fishing and duck hunting. Private clubs such as the Philadelphia Gunning Club attracted wealthy members from urban areas who could easily travel to the area by train. The magnate J. P. Morgan had a hunting hideaway on Spesutie Island. (Author's collection.)

THE ROAD TO OLD BALTIMORE. Old Baltimore was the original capital of Baltimore County when civilization settled at the shoreline and sailing was the best method of travel. A court was located there. Business was conducted there. The only modern photographs from the area were taken a few decades ago and show only a graveyard and the foundation of a building. (Courtesy U.S. Army.)

CORNFIELD, MICHAELSVILLE. A cornfield is just beginning to sprout. Buying land with farms included turned out to be a good deal for the army. Because horses were the main beasts of burden to build the new base and to transport officers, the army continued to farm some areas of the land for a few years to feed the animal—and human—workers. (Courtesy U.S. Army.)

MICHAELSVILLE FARM. A farmer tends his crops in the middle distance, and a cannery building and other structures are in the background. There is a sense of stillness and quiet in this portrait of bygone days, although there remain in Harford County a few places where stillness and quiet exist, and at night the light of a million stars shine clear in pitch-black skies. (Courtesy U.S. Army.)

Poole's Island Lighthouse APG, MD

POOLE'S ISLAND LIGHTHOUSE. The same island that gave its name to Poole's Island peaches boasts a lighthouse designed by John Donahoe. In fact, it is a twin to the lighthouse in Havre de Grace. This postcard commemorates the recent refurbishment of the historic structure by the army after it had been left to deteriorate for decades. (Courtesy the Historical Society of Harford County.)

VIEW OF GUNPOWDER RIVER SHORELINE. Although this photograph was taken after Edgewood Arsenal was established, the angle shows nothing but the shore and a home in the distance. This view is south of Maxwell Point looking south. (Courtesy the Historical Society of Harford County.)

VIEW OF BUSH RIVER. The Bush River, along with the Gunpowder, formed the natural boundaries of the Edgewood Peninsula. This view with a crude pier and a raft suggests lazy days of kids fishing and perhaps playing pirates like Tom Sawyer and Huck Finn. (Courtesy U.S. Army.)

ABERDEEN STREET VIEW. The army was not only buying secluded and expansive land and waters, it was also buying property that was on a rail line and that had several towns along its border. Aberdeen and Hall's Cross Roads, seen toward the top right of the map on page 19, were neighboring towns on either side of the railroad tracks. (Courtesy the Historical Society of Harford County.)

ABERDEEN SCHOOL. Along with the towns came schools. Aberdeen's school started the way most of Harford's small towns had, as a one-room schoolhouse. In 1908, this new eight-room schoolhouse was built for students from elementary through high school. After the army settled into Aberdeen, a larger school was needed, leading to the larger high school built in 1935 on Route 40. (Courtesy the Historical Society of Harford County.)

METHODIST EPISCOPAL CHURCH AND PARSONAGE, ABERDEEN. Churches were also important to the military. They provided a place of worship off base and often sponsored wholesome activities on base and off. Aberdeen had a selection of churches in various denominations for soldiers to choose from, such as this one built in 1893. (Courtesy James. R. Bierer.)

TRAIN STATION, ABERDEEN. Because of the importance of Harford County products to the major cities of Baltimore, Wilmington, Philadelphia, and New York, the railroad had long been established as a way of transporting people and freight. The army would take advantage of that infrastructure. (Courtesy Terry Noye.)

TRAIN STATION, PERRYMAN. The PW&B Railroad was the Philadelphia, Wilmington, and Baltimore line. The rail system grew as a series of small, often privately funded lines that were eventually bought and joined together to form large interstate lines. The PW&B eventually became part of the Pennsylvania Railroad. (Courtesy the Historical Society of Harford County.)

TRAIN STATION, BELCAMP. This station became a focal point for the Bata Shoe Company when its founder settled in Belcamp to establish the company there. Bata became a major supplier to the military when it introduced the process of vulcanization to coat soldiers' boots in rubber to make them waterproof. (Courtesy the Historical Society of Harford County.)

HOLLINGSWORTH WHEEL FACTORY. This factory flourished during the days when wagon wheels kept the economy turning, even into the early days of APG. It was located in the Winter's Run Valley and is now underwater; the entire valley area was flooded when the army built Atkisson Dam in 1943 to form a reservoir as the base ramped up growth to prepare for World War II. (Courtesy the Historical Society of Harford County.)

PERRY POINT, BIRD'S-EYE VIEW. The Cecil County town across the Susquehanna River from Havre de Grace became important for its Veteran's Administration hospital. The hospital took care of area vets from World War I who were injured or had disabilities from being gassed. Jerome Murphy recalls visiting his uncle, who lived the rest of his life at Perry Point after being blinded from mustard agent. (Courtesy the Historical Society of Harford County.)

EDGEWOOD AREA, BEFORE AND AFTER VIEW. The preceding photographs give a flavor of what Harford County looked like before the army began building the bases that would become known as Aberdeen Proving Ground and Edgewood Arsenal. But nothing quite drives home the extreme change in the landscape as these two photographs, taken by the army from roughly the same spot before construction began and after many of the plants in the Edgewood area had

been built. Colonel Ruggles undoubtedly made the right decision on behalf of the army when he chose to purchase the more than 70,000 acres of land and water in Harford County. By contrast, the 17,000-acre Kent Island site would not have been sufficient for the new proving ground. He did well for himself, too, being promoted to brigadier general and transferred to Washington in June 1918. (Courtesy U.S. Army.)

Maj. Gen. William L. Sibert. Sibert's goal was to develop the Edgewood area into a giant factory to produce finished artillery and mortar shells to ship out to troops in France. Very early on, he realized that Edgewood would also have to manufacture the poison gasses and chemical agents to fill those shells. In his role as director of the newly formed U.S. Army Chemical Warfare Service, Sibert was responsible for finding safe ways for soldiers in the field and in the air to use chemical weapons against the Germans. Sibert also had the belief that the United States should continue to research chemical weapons even after the war was over on November 11, 1918, as a more humane way of disabling and killing the enemy than with explosives and fire. The actual work of assembling resources and people to build Edgewood was put in the charge of its commanding officer, Col. William H. Walker. (Courtesy U.S. Army.)

Two

Chemical War
World War I

MAIN GATE, EDGEWOOD ARSENAL. "Have your button and identification card ready to show the guard," read the signs at the entrance in this World War I–era postcard image. In the entire history of APG, only two people have ever been shot at the gate, when a new guard on a month of 24-hour shifts gave two civilians in a car permission to drive through the gate and then shot at them. This chapter covers the construction of the shell-filling plants, chemical plants, ordnance testing, and the unforeseen deaths of 1918. (Courtesy the Historical Society of Harford County.)

TEMPORARY TROOP BARRACKS AND NEGRO BUNKS, MARCH 8, 1918. By the time construction began at Edgewood, the United States had entered the war and was playing catch up, especially in the new area of chemical weapons. Most of the troops who worked in the chemical plants lived in the wood and tar paper barracks visible on the right. Because the services were as segregated as American society, African American troops were given separate quarters. (Courtesy U.S. Army.)

LABOR BARRACKS IN SNOW. In the bitter cold, snow, and ice of the winter of 1917, civilian construction workers began building what was first called Gunpowder Neck Reservation and then later Edgewood Arsenal. They lived in the temporary wooden barracks seen here. The army eventually completed 16 permanent two-story troop barracks for enlisted men, while some officers lived in the abandoned farmhouses spread throughout the post. (Courtesy U.S. Army.)

MUSTARD AGENT PLANT UNDER CONSTRUCTION, JUNE 27, 1918. One of the first things to aid construction was the building of a spur from the main railroad line. The trains, visible on the left of the photograph, carried the materials for the roads, plants, and buildings into the base. The actual construction used the muscles of horses and men, as seen here. (Courtesy U.S. Army.)

CONSTRUCTING THE 20,000-KILOWATT POWER PLANT, AUGUST 20, 1918. This photograph shows the Bush River Power Plant. Its sister, the power plant of Shell Filling Plant No. 1, was the first permanent building completed at Edgewood—it is so sturdy that it stands today. It used coal brought in by train to produce power. Its four huge exhaust stacks were the immediately recognizable heart of the shell-filling and chemical plants. (Courtesy U.S. Army.)

CHLORINE PLANT SALT PREPARATION BUILDING, AUGUST 13, 1918. The entire process of producing the deadly oils, powders, liquids, and gasses that were used to fill ammunition shells had to be done on base, because private corporations couldn't justify the danger and cost of producing the huge amount of potentially lethal agents that the United States needed—agents already being used by the Germans and Allied forces in Europe. (Courtesy U.S. Army.)

CHLORINE PLANT, NELSON CELLS, AUGUST 1, 1918. Production began at Edgewood to make chlorine, phosgene, chloropicrin, and mustard agents. By the summer of 1918, the wide usage of gas masks was enough to make chlorine and chloropicrin unimportant as offensive gasses. Early in the war, French and British soldiers were told to protect themselves from gas by holding a urine-soaked cloth over their faces. (Courtesy U.S. Army.)

CHLOROPICRIN PLANT, JUNE 17, 1918. The plant looks shiny new, which it was—production had begun only a week before this photograph was taken. The phosgene plant was operational on March 1 and the chlorine plant on August 1. The giant condenser and steam stills took constant tending and, like most of the other plants, posed a constant danger to the men working it. (Courtesy U.S. Army.)

CHEMICAL LABORATORY, NOVEMBER 20, 1918. In addition to the chemical agent production and shell-filling operations, the post also completed its first chemical laboratory. The laboratory is made from distinctive terra cotta square tiles that became a hallmark of World War I structures on post. (Courtesy U.S. Army.)

GENERAL VIEW OF FILLING PLANTS, JUNE 20, 1918. The power plant is the heart of the complex. The train track runs alongside the building so the coal can be dumped directly into coal bunkers. The four wings comprise Shell Filling Plant No. 1, which became operational in April 1918. Soon after, 75-mm chemical-filled shells were being filled and readied for shipping in the shell dumps, or warehouses. (Courtesy U.S. Army.)

GENERAL VIEW OF THE PLANT, 1918. In response to the use of chemical weapons in Europe, the United States expanded the role of ordnance to include chemicals. The vision of Colonel Sibert is the reality of this photograph: plants that made chemicals and plants that took gunpowder, oils, and chemicals and filled all sizes of shells. (Courtesy U.S. Army.)

OFFICERS WHO FILLED THE FIRST SHELL. This group of officers was in charge of the shell-filling plants at Edgewood. Fourth from right is Lt. Col. Edwin M. Chance, who designed the shell-filling plants. He found the model for high-capacity filling plants in the milk, beer, and soda bottling industry. The numbers tell the rest of the story: 426,259 shells were filled, and over 300,000 were shipped to the troops. (Courtesy U.S. Army.)

BOMB FILLING. A soldier fills incendiary bombs—bombs intended to explode and create fires—with incendiary oil, a chemical that creates the fire when triggered by a charge. (Courtesy U.S. Army.)

GAS MASK CANISTER FILLING. Despite what appears, by today's standards, to be factory conditions that could be made a lot safer, only three people died at the operation at Edgewood as a result of direct exposure to chemicals. However, consider this account of early factory conditions by Maj. Hugo Hanson, the man who designed the mustard plant at Edgewood:

> Danger of serious injuries was always present. . . . During the first month there was no defensive apparatus except the gas mask, and we did not know the best reactive measures. The temperature [was] at one hundred, with the nauseating and burning fumes always in the air, it was only the thought of the value of our product in France that forced every pound of mustard gas from our first inadequate apparatus. [Even after conditions improved] there were always some fumes present, the continued action of which weakened the men's bronchial tubes and lungs. With the coming of the influenza epidemic the men were in no condition to resist its ravages and many died.

This postwar photograph shows civilians under conditions typical of the period. (Courtesy U.S. Army.)

SHELL DUMPS, SEPTEMBER 20, 1918. From these storage areas, bombs, grenades, mortars, and other ammunition were shipped out to the troops in Europe. Over 100,000 unshipped shells remained in inventory, unshipped due to a lack of parts. Occasional explosions occurred after the war among the stored shells, possibly from chemicals that leaked or became unstable. (Courtesy U.S. Army.)

LIVENS DRUM FILLING PLANT, INTERIOR, NOVEMBER 11, 1918. Livens projectors were mortars that shot out Livens drums filled with chemical agent. The British-developed weapon became the primary and most effective tool for ground forces. (Courtesy U.S. Army.)

PRESSURE TEST OF PHOSGENE CYLINDER, NOVEMBER 20, 1918. Before shells were packed for shipping or storage, each one was inspected for leakage. Because phosgene was a potentially fatal gas, the pressurized cylinders it was stored in underwent rigorous testing. Even though chemical production eventually ceased following the Armistice, the stock on hand had to be processed. (Courtesy U.S. Army.)

GAS MASK DRILL. Chemical workers had no protection except for the gas mask. But the mask was insufficient against mustard agent, which is not a gas—it is a brown oily substance that causes burns and blisters upon skin contact. Under the hottest of conditions it vaporizes, yet it is more than five times heavier than air, so it hugs the ground. Protective clothing had yet to be developed. (Courtesy U.S. Army.)

First Research Laboratory at Edgewood, Interior. Soldier-chemists conduct tests in Edgewood Arsenal's first research laboratory, built in 1918 to support the filling of shells with toxic chemicals manufactured on base. The best place to get an advanced degree in chemistry was, ironically, in Germany. Edgewood's commanding officer had a Ph.D. from the University of Goettingen and had taught chemical engineering at the Massachusetts Institute of Technology. (Courtesy U.S. Army.)

First Research Laboratory, November 20, 1918. Chemistry was the key to making the production plants work properly and as safely as possible. While trying to improve the production of mustard agent at Edgewood, Capt. Hugo Hanson experimented in the laboratory and in the plant up to 20 hours per day with only two officers to help. (Courtesy U.S. Army.)

41

TESTING ORDNANCE, MAIN FRONT. This extraordinary photograph gives a flavor of what it is like to stand at the main front testing ordnance with enough land stretching out in front to allow for firing from the largest guns in the arsenal. Here a gun mounted on a railcar is being tested. In fact, there was a railway artillery school that came to APG from Sandy Point. (Courtesy U.S. Army.)

GUN TESTING. Here a centrifugal gun is being tested. Although the Gatling gun was invented around the time of the Civil War, research on building multi-round-firing weapons continued. The gun showed here is being tested at the firing range on the main front at APG. (Courtesy U.S. Army.)

FOOTBALL SQUAD 1918. After the rigors of training and working closely with dangerous materials, organized sports were a good way to promote team spirit and blow off some of the pressures of wartime service. (Courtesy U.S. Army.)

CHAMPIONSHIP TEAM, 1918. Edgewood Arsenal's first baseball team won the Army-Navy League Championship in 1918. (Courtesy U.S. Army.)

U.S. FILLING STATION, DISPENSARY, AND EXCHANGE, MARCH 8, 1918. The canteen had the little luxuries of life for the soldier—a bar of chocolate, a souvenir for his girl back home, or "for the exquisite luxury of a pie such as mother never did make." Most prevalent, judging by the photograph below, was the sale of tobacco products. (Courtesy U.S. Army.)

POST EXCHANGE, OR CANTEEN. Edgewood Arsenal's exchange went into business on March 16, 1918, without a penny in cash. During the first year of operation, the canteen had a gross revenue of $453,000, most of which was derived from 5, 10, and 15¢ sales, and netted $100,000 profit that was spent on pianos, phonographs, books, billiard tables, band instruments, and athletic equipment for the arsenal's athletic teams. (Courtesy U.S. Army.)

DAY ROOM. The place for a recreational break, this room had a phonograph, books, and a billiard table, doubtless paid for by the earnings of the Post Exchange. (Courtesy U.S. Army.)

SIGNAL CORPS TELEPHONE EXCHANGE. The task of building the proving ground was shared by more than one group. The Engineers Corps designed and built many of the structures and helped lay the roads and infrastructure for the base, while the Signal Corps took charge of communications, as seen here. (Courtesy U.S. Army.)

ALL ATTENTION TO CHAPLAIN'S WORDS IN K. OF C. BUILDING.

COMMUNITY OUTREACH TO THE TROOPS. The Knights of Columbus was just one of many service organizations that came on base to entertain, edify, or just spend time with the troops. The structure in the scene here was actually the YMCA building. (Courtesy the Historical Society of Harford County.)

Volume One — ABERDEEN PROVING GROUND, MD., THURSDAY, OCT. 10, 1918. — Number Twenty-Three

Hospital Reports 500 Cases of "Flu"; Death Claims Nine Victims

With the epidemic of Spanish influenza still enveloping the country, conditions at Aberdeen Proving Ground continue on the upward trend, although the situation is not serious or alarming. Seven deaths during the past week make a total of nine since the scourge dealt its blow upon this camp. In comparison, however, with the number of deaths recorded in other camps we can be proud of the good work performed by the Medical Corps in alleviating the situation.

tion Company. The remains of Pvt. Halen, Cpt. Barnes, and Cpl. Davis were sent to their homes, while the body of Pvt. Maresi, who resided in Nevada City, Nev., was interred in the Reservation Burial Ground.

Shortly after the death of Cpl. Barnes a telegram was received from his mother saying that she and her daughter would arrive here Tuesday

Continued on Page Eleven.

125 MEN OUTGOING

Railway Artillery Men Get Rousing Send-off on Departure for France

Other things than guns are proved at the Aberdeen Proving Ground. And other stuff than ammunition is winning this war. These words might well have composed a cablegram to Kaiser Willie from the Railway Artillery and the Ordnance Engineering Schools last Thursday night.

During the afternoon preceding this Thursday evening, citizens of our shell-shaken community were questioningly watchful of mess hall 101. Irrespective of tradition, 101 bore no

when a banquet like that was in preparation and progress.

Order Received to Go Across.

It was about noon, by the Aberdeen City Hall clock, when the wires from Washington dotted off the long-expected yet aw-inspiring message. Meaning was breathed into the packs and belts and overseas equipment which the Railway Artillery has on their dusty and distant marches.

The school was going "Over There."

RAPID FIRE NEWSPAPER, OCTOBER 10, 1918. According to the main article, the news seemed not too bad, with only nine dead from the Spanish influenza epidemic of 1918. But the flu would reach its worst levels of lethality during the next six weeks, claiming 199 lives at Edgewood with over 1,300 sick in a hospital with 314 beds. Ironically, current research suggests that the main cause for the spread could have been crowds gathered for War Bond rallies. (Courtesy U.S. Army.)

American Troops in Parade — PARIS - 1918 4 th of July   A. P.

AMERICAN TROOPS ON PARADE IN PARIS, JULY 4, 1918. After Pres. Woodrow Wilson declared war on April 6, 1917, the United States took months to raise and train its army. In September 1918, the stage was set for the final battle with the Germans in the Meuse-Argonne offensive, 47 days of constant and determined fighting on both sides that led to the surrender of Germany and the Armistice of November 11, 1918. (Courtesy Marlene Herculson.)

GEN. JOHN J. "BLACKJACK" PERSHING. The victorious Pershing, at left, led the two million soldiers of the American Expeditionary Force in World War I. He is the only leader other than George Washington to be promoted to General of the Armies. The smiling officer in the center left of the photograph is George C. Marshall, who would play a vital role in World War II. (Courtesy the Historical Society of Harford County.)

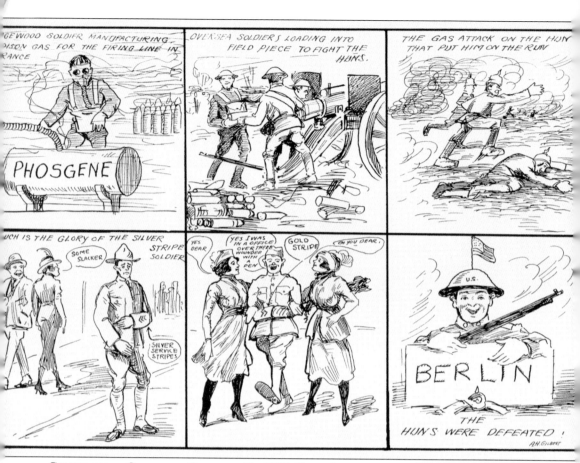

CELEBRATORY CARTOON, OCTOBER 10, 1918. From the same issue of *Rapid Fire*, this cartoon celebrates the certain defeat of Kaiser Wilhelm and the Germans. The war that had enmeshed Europe for two years before the United States became involved would soon be over, just 19 months after America's entry. Expecting Edgewood Arsenal to close, its commanding officer, Col. William H. Walker, reflected:

> "The idle plants of Edgewood Arsenal pay silent tribute to an organization of men unexcelled in unity of purpose, effectiveness of effort and loyalty to the cause they served. The satisfaction of having played a part in the design, the erection or the operation of this Arsenal is not less truly earned than that enjoyed by those who, on the battlefields of France, used the munitions here manufactured; nor is the satisfaction less because these splendid factories lie idle and the once busy highways are now deserted. The object for which the Arsenal was built, and to which its members here dedicated the best that was in them, has been attained. The war is won." (Courtesy U.S. Army.)

Three

THE READINESS
IS ALL
BETWEEN THE WARS

FIRST TRAFFIC ACCIDENT, EARLY 1920S. The traffic accident shown here occurred at APG. A similar accident at Edgewood resulted in the death of a pedestrian. This chapter covers some of the more spectacular mishaps, the changes at APG and Edgewood Arsenal after the war and through the 1920s and 1930s, the soldiers' pastimes, the creation of Fort Hoyle, and the growth of the civilian presence. (Courtesy U.S. Army.)

RESERVE OFFICERS TRAINING CORPS (ROTC) CAMP, 1922. The ROTC is learning about ordnance by doing—here ramming a projectile into a 14-inch gun. While the ordnance training for active-duty personnel was relocated to Watertown and Raritan Arsenals in New Jersey through the 1920s to early 1930s, the ROTC and Ordnance Reserve officers were trained at APG in the summers. (Courtesy the Historical Society of Harford County.)

TESTING A 16-INCH GUN. The physical reactions of the bystanders graphically show the visceral impact of the explosion that this huge gun channeled. The gun being tested at APG is fully four inches wider than the largest gun at Sandy Hook and was the largest gun in the American arsenal. (Courtesy U.S. Army.)

ORDNANCE TESTING, OCTOBER 8, 1923. This photograph answers the question of what happened to many of the fine old homes that families left when the government bought the land. Many were used for testing the effectiveness and accuracy of ordnance. The note on the photograph states, "Distruction [*sic*] of stairway completed by 300 lb. bomb at 25 feet." (Courtesy U.S. Army.)

ORDNANCE TESTING, OCTOBER 8, 1923. The same home as above has received irreparable damage to its kitchen—the heart of any home. The note states, "Arch of kitchen broken down by 300 lb. bomb at 25 feet." The bomb was set 25 feet from the structure and detonated by a static charge. (Courtesy U.S. Army.)

TRENCH WARFARE AREA BEFORE EXPLOSION. Trench warfare was the primary mode of combat for soldiers holding their positions in the field. They literally dug trenches to keep themselves out of firing range and to create a perimeter from which they could see and react to enemies' movements. This area on base allowed for testing the weapons of trench warfare. (Courtesy U.S. Army.)

CRATER FROM EXPLOSION, MARCH 12, 1919. One of the first in a series of spectacular explosions is documented in the next five photographs. It occurred in the trench warfare area (shown above) when someone left a batch of nitroglycerine to boil and then went to lunch along with his fellows. The pot caught fire, and four nearby storage sheds of gunpowder exploded. The damage was extensive. (Courtesy U.S. Army.)

TOWER AFTER EXPLOSION, MARCH 12, 1919. The tower allowed for the sighting of the flight and impact of artillery shells. Here it is a casualty of the explosion. Fifteen people were injured, though there were no fatalities. There were other ordnance accidents, however, that did result in deaths. (Courtesy U.S. Army.)

TRAIN TRACKS AND DEBRIS FROM EXPLOSION, MARCH 12, 1919. Other accidents included the detonation of stored artillery shells. Despite living a quarter-mile away from the grounds on the other side of the fence, a young boy was thrown into convulsions from the force of the blast. (Courtesy U.S. Army.)

MACHINE SHOP AFTER EXPLOSION, MARCH 12, 1919. Considering the number of shells produced and the amount of ordnance in various stages of assembly, transport, and storage, the wonder is that more calamitous accidents did not occur. (Courtesy the Historical Society of Harford County.)

MACHINE SHOP CLOSE-UP, MARCH 12, 1919. In just the first month of operation, the proving ground fired 5,032 rounds, in addition to dropping its first bomb—from a balloon at the site of Old Baltimore. (Courtesy the Historical Society of Harford County.)

SMOKE DISPERSAL TEST.
The testing of effective
ways of to release smoke
and gasses never came
to a stop at APG and
Edgewood. (Courtesy
U.S. Army.)

**LT. WENDELL K.
PHILLIPS.** Phillips, a pilot
at APG, was involved
in one of the few plane
accidents at the base.
The old and new Phillips
Airfields are named in
his honor. (Courtesy
the Historical Society
of Harford County.)

HANDLEY-PAGE AIRCRAFT. The Handley-Page aircraft was the World War I equivalent of the B-1 bomber. Another accident occurred on May 30, 1921, when a faulty mechanism allowed the release of a 50-pound bomb from a de Havilland bomber as it was taking off. Five workers died and 11 were injured. (Courtesy the Historical Society of Harford County.)

CRASH, JUNE 5, 1923. Lieutenant Phillips was killed in this accident at APG. This view of the accident shows the inherent danger in testing new weapons and vehicles. Of course, without the extensive testing of equipment, and without the brave volunteers involved in the testing process, the main mission of the proving ground could not happen. (Courtesy U.S. Army.)

4679

FIRST GAS REGIMENT MANEUVERS, NOVEMBER 1927. Mules are being used to draw carts that likely hold Stokes mortars. Although the weapon, when broken into its three component parts, was designed to be carried by soldiers, the weight of the steel pieces was still formidable: the barrel (tube) weighed 43 pounds, the base plate 28 pounds, and the bipod 37 pounds, for a total of 108 pounds. (Courtesy U.S. Army.)

FIELD ARTILLERY HORSES. The 6th Artillery, stationed at Fort Hoyle, was able to take advantage of the latest protection, such as gas masks for their horses. The horses were vital for drawing heavy pieces of artillery in the field. Improvements in motor vehicles would make horses less important in coming wars. (Courtesy U.S. Army.)

FIRST GAS REGIMENT ON THE ROAD, NOVEMBER 1927. A motorcycle and sidecar take front and center in this photograph—there must be an officer about. The horses draw ammunition, equipment, and artillery while the men of the 1st Gas regiment march along, although they seem to be taking a break or waiting for orders to move along. (Courtesy U.S. Army.)

CHEMICAL WARFARE RESERVE OFFICERS. The men here receive instructions in the use of Livens projectors, a kind of mortar that fired chemical cylinders, usually filled with phosgene. To create a gas cloud, a bank of the projectors was fired. The cylinders would land, empty their contents, and collectively form a gas cloud that could overcome the enemy. (Courtesy U.S. Army.)

ROTC IN TRAINING. The men are being drilled in the use of the Stokes mortar, a three-part weapon. The 51-inch-long smoothbore tube or barrel had a 4-inch diameter. This had a metal end cap that fit into a flat base plate. The barrel was supported by two legs, or a bipod, that adjusted for ranges of 100 to 1,100 yards, firing an 25-pound, high-explosive shell. (Courtesy U.S. Army.)

CHEMICAL AGENT TESTING. As with any kind of testing, many different recordings were taken to fully understand the physical mechanisms involved. Here the subject breathes from the interior of a chamber into a spirometer—an instrument that records the amount and the rate of air that is breathed in and out over a specified time. (Courtesy U.S. Army.)

MUSTARD AGENT TEST CHAMBER, JULY 1, 1929. This test chamber exposes a protectively clothed man to HS (mustard agent) vapor. The list of parts is: (1) fan; (2) tuner; (3) rheostat; (4) HS chamber; (5) man operating the apparatus for drawing mustardized air at a definite speed through the charcoal sampling tube; and (6) charcoal sampling tube. The fan produces a continuous flow of air through the tunnel, which contains a receptacle with HS heated electrically. (Courtesy U.S. Army.)

PROTECTIVE CLOTHING TESTING, JUNE 19, 1929. This photograph and the next document tests of impregnated clothing against turpentine vapors in a large tunnel. Turpentine vapor was used instead of HS vapor. The parts are: (1) blower house and (2) fume exit stack. Men in protective suits are about to enter the tunnel for testing. (Courtesy U.S. Army.)

INSIDE THE TUNNEL, JUNE 19, 1929. The clothing being tested is made of cloth that has been impregnated with chemicals to withstand penetration by mustard vapors. The men stand inside the tunnel near an entrance door at the exhaust end of the tunnel ready for the test to begin. The dark squares on the suits are impregnated cloth samples for testing. (Courtesy U.S. Army.)

OUTDOOR TESTING, JULY 1, 1929. Again, a protectively clothed man stands ready for testing in an HS chamber—this time, an outdoor test. Once the most protective cloth was created, various designs were tested that allowed for flexibility while staying safe. (Courtesy U.S. Army.)

FORT HOYLE, OFFICERS' GATE. An area between APG and Edgewood Arsenal was carved out for the transfer in 1922 of the 6th Field Artillery. One of the legacies of Fort Hoyle was the officers' housing. The 6th Artillery was moved from Regiment Edgewood in 1940 to make room for the expansion of the base in light of the threat of war. (Courtesy Bill Walsh.)

FORT HOYLE, HORSES AND STABLES. Another legacy of Fort Hoyle was Riding Hall (not pictured), built in 1938 two years before the 6th left the area. Intended as an indoor facility for the training of horses, the hall was later repurposed as an auditorium and renamed Hoyle Auditorium to serve Edgewood Arsenal. (Courtesy Bill Walsh.)

BAND. The 1st Gas Regiment Band appears with former members of the 1st Gas Regiment in this ceremonial photograph. (Courtesy U.S. Army.)

BASEBALL GAME AT APG. Baseball was not just the national pastime, it was the neighborhood pastime. In Harford County alone, teams of young boys often grew into teams of young men with minor-league status. In a rural area such as Harford, baseball was often the glue that held together friendships and communities. (Courtesy U.S. Army.)

BATHING PIER. This bathing or recreation pier on the Gunpowder River was conveniently located near the barracks of the 1st Gas Regiment at Edgewood. Some of the Edgewood buildings are visible in the background. (Courtesy U.S. Army.)

DAY ROOM OF COMPANY D, 1ST GAS REGIMENT. A piano and billiard table, funded by the Post Exchange, provide some of the recreational possibilities for the men. (Courtesy U.S. Army.)

LIBRARY. The 1st Gas Regiment at Edgewood had its own library as a place to read—but mainly to study for those chemical warfare exams. (Courtesy U.S. Army.)

MESS HALL. Enlisted men are pictured at mess in Company D, First Gas Regiment. Note the spartan room reminiscent of mess at Fort Hancock—simple tables and stools, minus the tin ceiling. (Courtesy U.S. Army.)

TESTING STUDENTS, MARCH 18, 1925. Students take an examination on chemical warfare problems in a Chemical Warfare School classroom in Building 250. (Courtesy U.S. Army.)

MOTOR POOL GARAGE. As with their guns, mechanics were expected to disassemble any part of a vehicle and reassemble it as training for field action. (Courtesy U.S. Army.)

MACHINE SHOP TRAINING. Enlisted men receive training at the Machine Shop at Edgewood Arsenal. Notice the terra cotta of the walls, typical of World War I construction at Edgewood. (Courtesy U.S. Army.)

CHEMICAL WARFARE CLASS DEMONSTRATION, OCTOBER 30, 1924. This class in physical lab at the Chemical Warfare School is watching a demonstration of an electrical exploder that fires 500 Livens projectors, which were mortar tubes that shot 30-pound cylinders of pressurized gas about a mile toward enemy lines, creating chemical clouds of gas. The projector was named for its inventor, the British army captain William Livens. (Courtesy U.S. Army.)

EDGEWOOD ARSENAL EMPLOYEES, DECEMBER 1923. These employees from the Executive Division are part of a coming trend of increasing civilian employees on base, especially with the onset of World War II. (Courtesy U.S. Army.)

PAYDAY AT EDGEWOOD ARSENAL. In this c. 1921 photograph, wartime workers at Edgewood Arsenal line up at post headquarters to receive their pay, perhaps most of which was earmarked for payment on their newly acquired Model Ts or to hand over to waiting wives. (Courtesy U.S. Army.)

ORDNANCE DEPARTMENT, A. P. G.
27118 - 10/9/30.
A group around the 16-inch Gun.

GROUP PHOTOGRAPH ON A 16-INCH GUN, OCTOBER 9, 1930. Groups visiting the ordnance area of APG were allowed to have their photographs taken on the big gun. (Courtesy U.S. Army.)

MEMORIAL SERVICE, JUNE 4, 1925. Pictured is the unveiling of the memorial tablet at Edgewood Arsenal dedicated to the officers and men of the 1st Gas Regiment who died in service during World War I. (Courtesy U.S. Army.)

Visit of American Chemical Society, April 26, 1924. Members of the American Chemical Society are transported around Edgewood Arsenal via the Toonerville Trolley. (Courtesy U.S. Army.)

Lunch at APG, April 26, 1924. The American Chemical Society made annual visits to Edgewood Arsenal. Here the group enjoys an outdoor luncheon. (Courtesy U.S. Army.)

ORDNANCE DEPARTMENT, A. P. G.
Neg. #20114, 10/3/24. 6th. Annu
Meeting, Army Ord. Assn. At Mai
Proof Front. Demonstration of T
Mobile Gun Carriages. Front

MAIN FRONT VISITORS, OCTOBER 3, 1924. Members of the Army Ordnance Association visit the main front of the proving ground during their sixth annual meeting, watching a demonstration of tank mobile gun carriages. The men seem right at home as they perch on the huge equipment. Edgewood and Aberdeen were favorite spots for such meetings and over the years welcomed professional groups. (Courtesy U.S. Army.)

AERIAL VIEW OF EDGEWOOD ROAD'S ENTRY TO APG. Train tracks run from the top to bottom of the photograph, and the town of Edgewood is to the left. This 1919 view shows how close the tiny town was to the Edgewood Arsenal. (Courtesy U.S. Army.)

HOSTESS HOUSE. This building served as hospitality rooms for visitors in the early 1920s and then became officers' quarters. (Courtesy U.S. Army.)

Four

A CITY OF 30,000

CHEMICAL WARFARE SCHOOL ACTIVITIES, AUGUST 1, 1929. The class, dressed in protective clothing, listens to a talk by the assistant commandant of the school on the use of chemical agents used with airplanes in time of war. They must have been warm—notice the Queen Anne's Lace in bloom in the field at right. This chapter shows the preparations for World War II. The training of soldiers was primary, but the war brought to APG a huge increase in funding for projects in the research of ballistics, x-rays, and supersonics, and the applications of that research. The campus was changing, with new buildings for the Ordnance and Chemical Commands and barracks and classrooms to hold more than 100,000 military personnel from all services who would come for training in ordnance and chemical warfare. To ready the infrastructure of the base for the influx of soldiers, more of everything was needed—more power, more water, and more space. (Courtesy U.S. Army.)

CHEMICAL-LOADING CRANE, JANUARY 4, 1939. Research and testing was not limited to weapons. In this case, the problem to solve was how to hoist and support 55-gallon steel drums during the filling of airplane chemical spray tanks. This crane was the answer, provided by the Munitions Development Division in December 1938. (Courtesy U.S. Army.)

GAS ATTACK DRILL. Once the tanks on the plane above were filled with chemicals, the plane could run a gas attack drill, such as here. Sometimes the gas was a real chemical if suits were being tested; otherwise colored smoke might be used for readiness drills. (Courtesy U.S. Army.)

CHEMICAL MORTAR SQUAD, JANUARY 15, 1937. The mortar was the primary offensive weapon during World War I and II and continues to be so. Soldiers here use a hand-drawn cart to carry around their munitions and launchers. (Courtesy U.S. Army.)

DECONTAMINATION DRILL. Soldiers are trained to clean up the sludgy goo that is mustard agent, neutralizing the agent on the ground by shoveling a bleach solution on it and mixing the two together. Protective clothing keeps the soldiers safe. The bleach-filled sandbox was the last step for the soldiers to neutralize agent that clung to the feet. (Courtesy U.S. Army.)

ROAD REPAIR, EDGEWOOD ARSENAL. This 1919 view shows the time-honored method of repairing roads—human labor. With the coming explosion of construction, heavy machinery would certainly be called into action. (Courtesy U.S. Army.)

ATKISSON DAM. The reservoir that formed from the damming up of Winter's Run helped supply the base during World War II. After the war, the army declared a major portion of the land surplus, including much of the reservoir area itself. The county turned the property into Harford Glen, which has been a nature center for generations of Harford's schoolchildren. (Courtesy U.S. Army.)

MAIN FRONT, MUNSON TEST AREA. The test area was renamed in 1944 for 2d Lt. Max Leroy Munson, who was killed on November 10, 1941, at the Phillips Field Test Area, Automotive Division, while conducting tests. (Courtesy U.S. Army.)

TWO-BAY GUN SHELTER AND LOOKOUT. Building 684 was completed in July 1942 for $12,900. This and the next six photographs are from an inventory showing a number of new construction and improvement projects made during a frenzy of new construction and leasing of outside land in preparation for, or approved in the time of, World War II. (Courtesy U.S. Army.)

ASSEMBLY PLANT, WATER RANGE. Building M635 was completed in May 1943 at a cost of $47,300. (Courtesy U.S. Army.)

INDUSTRIAL ASSEMBLY AND REPAIR BUILDING. Building 525 was completed in October 1942 at a cost of $697,400. (Courtesy U.S. Army.)

ONE-MILLION-VOLT X-RAY BUILDING. Building 449 was completed in December 1945 for $265,125. The work done here led directly to nuclear research, still in its early stages despite the use of nuclear bombs against Japan. (Courtesy U.S. Army.)

SUPERSONIC WIND TUNNEL BUILDING, BUILDING 120. Dr. Edwin Hubble served at APG during the war in the Ballistics Research Laboratory and developed the first supersonic wind tunnel. The Hubble Space Telescope was named for him. (Courtesy U.S. Army.)

BALLISTICS RESEARCH LABORATORY BUILDING SITE, MARCH 5, 1940. This before-and-after set of photographs shows how quickly projects were completed in light of the world conflicts. In just about a year's time, the vital Ballistics Research Laboratory, or BRL as it is called, was built. (Courtesy U.S. Army.)

BALLISTICS RESEARCH LABORATORY BUILDING, MAY 1, 1941. In this building, some of the most brilliant minds would conduct research to bring about advances as varied as the supersonic wind tunnel and the first electronic digital computer. (Courtesy U.S. Army.)

Five

SOLDIERS AND
CITIZENS TOGETHER
WORLD WAR II

ORDNANCE TRAINING CENTER POSTCARD. The cartoons on the lower sides of the card suggest that civilians go into training and come out soldiers—or that boys become men. Intended to give comfort to parents and girlfriends back home, this card emphasized the softer side of ordnance training. This chapter celebrates the civilians, especially the women, who took the dangerous jobs previously performed by military personnel. As the war was being fought in Europe and in the Pacific, every man—and woman who would sign up to go—was needed in battle. (Courtesy the Historical Society of Harford County.)

No. 639   Obstacle Course—Ordnance Training Center—Aberdeen Proving Ground, Md.

OBSTACLE COURSE, ORDNANCE TRAINING CENTER. One of the first orders that new army recruits receive is to write home to tell their families they are fine. Soldiers are provided with postcards such as this one showing daily activities on base to the folks back home. (Courtesy the Historical Society of Harford County.)

No. 635   Obstacle Course—Ordnance Training Center—Aberdeen Proving Ground, Md.

OBSTACLE COURSE, ORDNANCE TRAINING CENTER. The sender, a new recruit, writes, "Just a line to let you know I haven't forgotten you. This Army life is a busy life, especially the first few weeks at least." (Courtesy the Historical Society of Harford County.)

70469

MAKING BUNKS, ORDNANCE TRAINING CENTER. The long lines of two-story, wooden barracks at APG, the last of their kind still standing in the United States, were recently torn down. (Courtesy Terry Noye.)

No. 632   Company Street—Ordnance Training Center—Aberdeen Proving Ground, Md.

COMPANY STREET, ORDNANCE TRAINING CENTER. One private writes home, "Dear Ma, Did a big washing Friday night wish you could have been here to help. Old fashioned scrub board. Front is exact picture of platoon I & 64 other fellows live in. Helped build a boat house all day. Weather is terrible here about 15 degrees in morning & about 55 in afternoon & mud every place." (Courtesy the Historical Society of Harford County.)

One of the Telephone Centers maintained for the armed forces at
ABERDEEN PROVING GROUND - MARYLAND
by The Chesapeake & Potomac Telephone Co. of Baltimore City

TELEPHONE CENTER, APG. A promotional postcard shows the local phone company's support for the troops. A postcard home was free to the military; a phone call home was expensive—and restricted when on base. (Courtesy the Historical Society of Harford County.)

ABERDEEN, MD., CORNER BEL AIR AVE. AND PHILADELPHIA BOULEVARD   OB-H1338

ABERDEEN, CORNER OF BEL AIR AND PHILADELPHIA ROADS. A trip to town might include seeing a movie at the New Theater. On this postcard, postmarked 1943, the marquee shows Merle Oberon starring in the 1940 movie *Till We Meet Again*. (Courtesy Nancy M. Sheetz.)

HARFORD RESTAURANT ADVERTISEMENT. Although formal in tone, this 1943 advertisement must have sounded appealing to a soldier wishing for some homemade cooking. (Courtesy U.S. Army.)

CARTOON FROM THE ABERDEEN PROVING GROUNDHOG MAGAZINE. The war brought together more than GIs and their gals. The men and women on production lines at APG and Edgewood were part of something new in American society. People from all different walks of life came to help the war effort and found themselves working side by side. And sometimes that led to romance. (Courtesy U.S. Army.)

" They met on the assembly line.   It was love at first bomb sight."

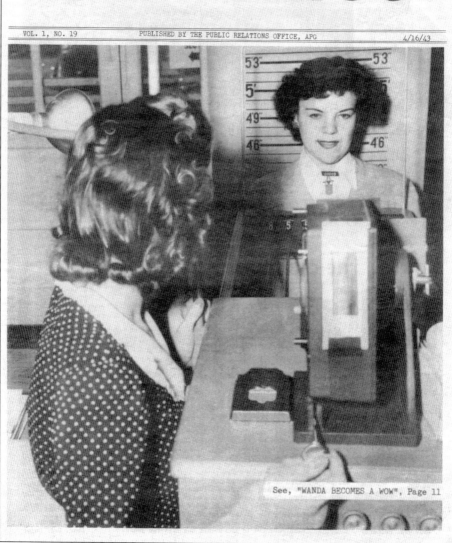

The Aberdeen Proving GROUNDHOG

VOL. 1, NO. 19   PUBLISHED BY THE PUBLIC RELATIONS OFFICE, APG   4/16/43

See, "WANDA BECOMES A WOW", Page 11

COVER OF THE ABERDEEN PROVING GROUNDHOG MAGAZINE, APRIL 16, 1943. The groundhog is the mascot of APG because there are groundhogs everywhere at APG. They are large—about the size of a large cat or a small dog—but they keep to themselves and don't usually cause problems. Many of the native animals have been disrupted in their habitats from explosions and chemicals, but some, including eagles, are making a comeback. From the very beginning of APG, communication among the troops was important for morale. And the men stepped up by publishing the military equivalent of a campus newspaper or newsletter. The edition of *Rapid Fire* on page 46 is the very first example. In October 1942, the first issue of the *Aberdeen Proving Groundhog* came off the presses. Today's *APG News* stands proudly in a long line of army publications. (Courtesy U.S. Army.)

FORT OSBORNE. One of the satellite outposts of property either bought or leased by the army, Fort Osborne was located on the south side of Wesleyan Chapel Road and used for field experience by the Officer Candidate School. In addition, bivouac training activities were held in camps located throughout Harford and Cecil Counties in Betterton, Belcamp, Carsins Run, Elk Neck Park, and off Wesleyan Chapel Road, among other places. (Courtesy U.S. Army.)

FIFTY-FIFTH AMMUNITION CORPS. This photograph is undated but documents that the duties of African American servicemen in a segregated society tended to be in the more labor-intensive roles. Here, for example, the men are caught in a relaxed moment outside the ammunition depot office, where their normal duties included the dangerous job of loading and unloading ammunition. (Courtesy U.S. Army.)

HUMOROUS POSTCARD. The sad sack soldier is a comic character in all wars in all countries. He was the embodiment of all that seemed to go wrong for the soldiers, although, like Beetle Bailey in today's comics, he has his occasional and hard-won moments of glory. (Courtesy the Historical Society of Harford County.)

MOTHER PINNING AWARD ON SOLDIER. Part of the ceremonies for graduating officers was to have mom pin on the medal—and maybe make a few final adjustments to make sure the uniform looked perfect. From his first postcard home to graduation, the soldier kept his family informed and involved. (Courtesy U.S. Army.)

GRADUATION AT THE ORDNANCE TRAINING SCHOOL. The three fieldstone buildings of the Ordnance School were constructed between 1938 and 1940, primarily with funds from the Works Progress Administration (WPA) and the Public Works Administration (PWA). They were designed by Capt. Elmer Walters of the Quartermaster Corps to create a setting more like a college campus than a utilitarian military post. The buildings held facilities for instruction, barracks, mess halls, and administration. It was the spearhead project that saw the expansion of APG as more land was purchased or leased and many more buildings added. The result of the expansion is in the numbers: during the war years alone—between 1942 and 1945—more than 75,000 men received training at APG. (Courtesy U.S. Army.)

Signal Drill, Bainbridge, Md.

BAINBRIDGE NAVAL TRAINING CENTER GRADUATES. To the north of Aberdeen was its naval counterpart. The U.S. Naval Training Center Bainbridge was activated on October 1, 1942, and deactivated on March 31, 1976, having trained over 500,000 navy recruits, with thousands more receiving specialty training. Situated in Cecil County on the northeast bank of the Susquehanna River, the facility began with the buildings from the Jacob Tome Institute School for Boys and added over 500 buildings to house and train more than 20,000 men and women at a time during World War II and a peak of 55,000 during the Korean War. The base was named for Commodore William Bainbridge, commander of the frigate USS *Constitution* and founder of the first naval training school. (Courtesy Ed Ward.)

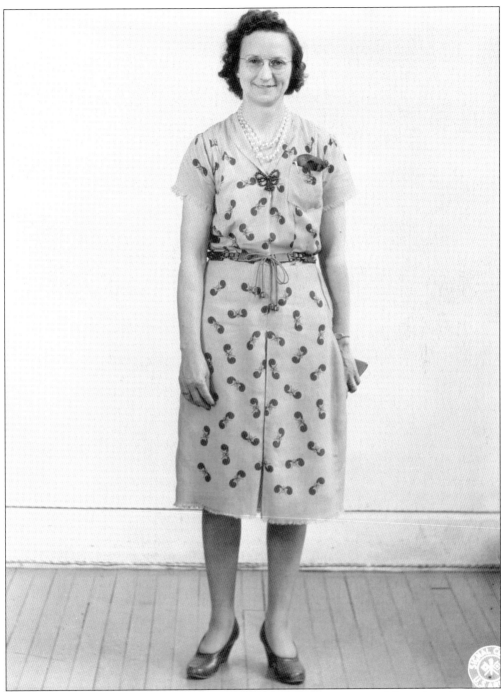

DRESS MADE FROM SCARVES, JULY 1944. During the war, citizens practiced the enforced rationing of food, gas, and goods, saved metal and tin foil, and used less of just about everything so the soldiers could have more. This dress, made from Chemical Warfare Service scarves, is an example of frugality that was commended. The report read, "Mrs. Blanche Lane, Building 509, fashioned a dress from four CWS scarves. Total cost of dress: 4 scarves @ 50 cents each: $2, 1 blue belt: 39 cents, 1 spool yellow cotton: 5 cents, 1 salvaged zipper." (Courtesy U.S. Army.)

CIVILIANS TAKE ON DANGEROUS DUTY. At APG and Edgewood Arsenal, the hazardous jobs had to be given over to a primarily civilian workforce because the soldiers were needed to fight on the two fronts. This next series of 20 photographs documents various jobs at APG working with chemicals and ammunition. Here workers assemble burster tubes for gas tank igniters at Building 601 on May 2, 1945. (Courtesy U.S. Army.)

CHEMICAL LAB WORK. During the war years, everyday folks stepped up to run tests, pour chemicals, mix explosives, fill shells, make and repair vehicles and weapons systems, and continue the support jobs on base that civilians had always done, from baking and cleaning to tailoring and shoe repairing. At Building 87, Earl Coy (left), George Stansbury (center), and Harold Smith (right) work in the Analytical Laboratory on May 2, 1945. (Courtesy U.S. Army.)

EQUIPPING A NELSON CELL. James Gummert deposits a diaphragm in one of the Nelson cells in the chlorine plant on May 2, 1945. (Courtesy U.S. Army.)

BRINE TREATMENT. Tending to the brine treatment in the chlorine plant are James Williams (left) and Harrison Butler on May 2, 1945. (Courtesy U.S. Army.)

CLUSTER BOMB MANUFACTURING. No, those levers aren't attached to slot machines. These ladies are in Building 77B clustering the bomblets that make up M77 cluster bombs. (Courtesy U.S. Army.)

FILLING SPOTTING CHARGES. This unnamed worker in Building 82 fills spotting charges with FS, a smoke-producing chemical. Spotting charges are used for ordnance practice to see the accuracy of the bomb—the charge flashes and produces white smoke that helps illuminate the blast site. (Courtesy U.S. Army.)

CHECKING LEVELS. Raymond Dawson checks the levels in the Chlorine Evaporation Building on May 2, 1945. (Courtesy U.S. Army.)

CHARTS A-OK. James Howard checks a chart to make sure things are proceeding smoothly in Building 701 on May 2, 1945. (Courtesy U.S. Army.)

FUSING BOMBS. In Building 701, this careful, patient lady fuses M77 bombs—cluster bomblets—on May 2, 1945. (Courtesy U.S. Army.)

CHECKING THE PRESSURE. CPO Joseph West works in the Liquefaction Room of the Chlorine Plant on May 2, 1945. (Courtesy U.S. Army.)

NEED MORE PAINT. Joseph D. Brooks, a spray painter, opens a drum of paint in Building 509 in August 1945. Painting bombs was a crucial last step on the bomb production line. Paint color and painted-on lines and marks identified the type of bomb—to distinguish, for example, a smoke bomb made for ordnance practice from one made for battle. (Courtesy U.S. Army.)

ROLL OUT THE TON CONTAINERS. These fellows—names not listed—are busy at Building 644 moving ton containers of chlorine on May 2, 1945. Raised tracks allow some ease of movement of the containers, which hold one ton of liquid but also weigh over 1,000 pounds when empty. (Courtesy U.S. Army.)

BOMB STORAGE. Bombs away—hot off the production line. These unnamed fellows carefully arrange bombs in Building 60 on November 25, 1944, as they are brought in on the forklift. The phosgene (CG)–filled 1,000-pound M79 and 500-pound M78 bombs, along with 7.2-inch rockets, fill every available inch of floor. Please observe the "No Smoking" sign. (Courtesy U.S. Army.)

PAINTING SHELLS. In Building 509, the ladies are painting and marking 5-inch naval shells for clear identification. (Courtesy U.S. Army.)

PAINTING GRENADES. Also in Building 509 are these women, who are painting and marking grenades for gas tank igniters. (Courtesy U.S. Army.)

REWORKING SHELLS. The woman in the foreground is reworking a 4.2-inch chemical mortar shell in Building 84 on February 9, 1945. (Courtesy U.S. Army.)

KEEPING IT COOL. Checking on a refrigeration unit are James Williams and Melba Redmon. (Courtesy U.S. Army.)

ASSEMBLING SHELLS. This group in Building 84 assembles 4.2-inch chemical mortar shells with HE. (Courtesy U.S. Army.)

SANDBAGS FOR SAFETY. Another man in Building 84 also assembles 4.2-inch chemical mortar shells. The bank of sandbags reveals that the assembly process could have some danger associated with it. (Courtesy U.S. Army.)

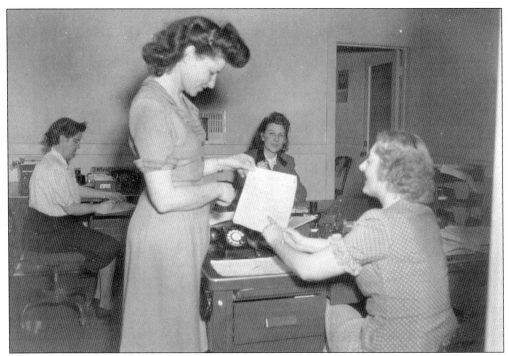

OFFICE DUTY. Maybe just a tad more peaceful than the bomb factories on a hectic day, the personnel office in Building 715 employs, from left to right, Elsie Hopkins, Mary Miskelly, Ida Goldberg, and Freda Bull. (Courtesy U.S. Army.)

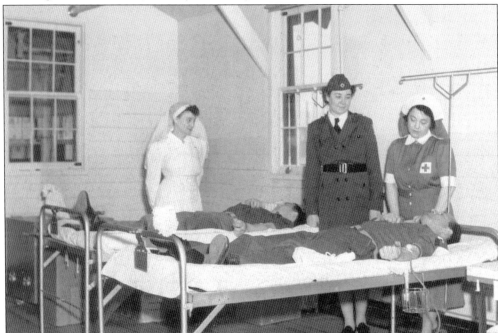

GIVING BLOOD. In time of war, nothing is as important as giving blood to the Red Cross. Here, soldiers show how it's done. Almost every phase of life saw sacrifices willingly made by those who were left behind. (Courtesy U.S. Army.)

MOTOR GARAGE. During World War II, the sheer numbers of men overseas, with the resulting lack of men at home, forced women to come to the forefront in all roles on base. They fabricated, repaired, and maintained equipment and weapons systems. They took over in all clerical functions, not just the most menial. And they were vital in running the first computers. (Courtesy the Historical Society of Harford County.)

MOTOR GARAGE, GROUP PHOTOGRAPH. Despite working at some of the most physically demanding of jobs, women also had to work hard to get some changes made: Eleanor Roosevelt and other leading women of the day mounted a media campaign to get slacks adopted as acceptable work wear for women. (Courtesy the Historical Society of Harford County.)

TANK REPAIR CREW. Women in overalls fine-tune a tank—just one of the many traditionally male and military roles that civilian women filled on base during World War II. (Courtesy the Historical Society of Harford County.)

TANK REPAIR CREW, GROUP PHOTOGRAPH. These gals knew the tanks inside and out and kept them in tip-top condition. (Courtesy the Historical Society of Harford County.)

ORDNANCE MUSEUM, BUILDING 314. The Ordnance Museum was established soon following World War I. Starting in 1919, the museum's collection was housed in this sprawling metal building that had been shipped from France. The museum opened to the public in 1927. For security reasons, the museum was closed during World War II. (Courtesy the Historical Society of Harford County.)

ORDNANCE MUSEUM, BUILDING 314, INTERIOR. From 1919 until 1968, the Ordnance Museum remained in this building. During World War II and the Korean War, the collection was raided for scrap metal, but it was also used for ordnance technical intelligence studies, indoctrination in all phases of ordnance, and other purposes. (Courtesy the Historical Society of Harford County.)

EQUIPMENT AND WEAPONS STOCKPILE. At the end of World War I, most of the equipment and weapons that had gone unused were shipped back to the States. Some of that stockpile, as well as some of the best examples of enemy and Allied weaponry and supplies, became incorporated into the collection of the Ordnance Museum. (Courtesy the Historical Society of Harford County.)

THE MUSEUM MOVES OUT, MARCH 1967. For financial reasons, the army would not allow the footprint of Building 314 to change, but the building was essentially reconstructed with new materials and with a completely different appearance. (Courtesy the Historical Society of Harford County.)

MAIN FRONT, MARCH 9, 1945. This photograph of the Ordnance Research and Development Center was taken looking west from A Tower. (Courtesy U.S. Army.)

GENERAL STILWELL AND THE FLAMETHROWER. On a visit to APG in May 1945, Gen. Joseph Stilwell tries out a flamethrower at the main front. (Courtesy U.S. Army.)

FDR at APG, September 30, 1940. Presidents Franklin Roosevelt and Harry Truman visited APG and Edgewood Arsenal. For his visit, Roosevelt was accompanied by Maryland governor Herbert O'Conor and Librarian of Congress Archibald MacLeish, among others. FDR arrived by yacht by way of the Chesapeake Bay and went on by car to visit the anti-aircraft range and main front at APG and then on to Edgewood and Fort Meade. Under the Roosevelt administration, APG added or refurbished many buildings utilizing funds from various federal programs, such as the Federal Emergency Works Administration (FEWA). The Civilian Conservation Corps (CCC) improved ranges and fields. And another thousand acres of land was added to APG, much of it cornfields. (Courtesy the Historical Society of Harford County.)

ARMY-NAVY "E" AWARD, CHEMICAL WARFARE CENTER, NOVEMBER 23, 1942. The Army-Navy "E" Award was the top award given for munitions production. As such, it celebrated the civilian workers, especially, who did most of the production work at Edgewood during the war. Addresses were given by, among others, Maj. Gen. Milton A. Reckord, after whom the National Guard armory in Bel Air is named. (Courtesy U.S. Army.)

You are cordially invited to attend

the presentation of the

Army-Navy Production Award

to

Edgewood Arsenal

for

Excellence in War Production

on the afternoon of November twenty-third

nineteen hundred and forty-two

at three-fifteen o'clock

at

Edgewood, Maryland

ENTERING HOYLE AUDITORIUM. Millard E. Tydings, senior United States senator from Maryland, and Brig. Gen. R. L. Avery, U.S. Army, commanding general of Edgewood Arsenal, gave addresses as well. Tydings had represented the interests of the Michaelsville families and Aberdeen business owners who sued the government for more money following the 1917 land purchase. Tydings finally got a settlement for the people—30 years later. (Courtesy U.S. Army.)

ARMY-NAVY "E" AWARD BANNER. The raising of the "E" Award banner features the color guard and William Reilly of the Property Division. Edgewood won this award each year during the war. For this first award, in 1942, over 30,000 people turned out. (Courtesy U.S. Army.)

PRESENTATION OF ARMY WAR BOND FLAGS AT EDGEWOOD ARSENAL ON JANUARY 17, 1944. Another award for Edgewood, the War Bond "T" flag is presented by Maj. Gen. William Porter, chief of the Chemical Warfare Service. (Courtesy U.S. Army.)

DANCE AT THE ORDNANCE SCHOOL'S 40TH ANNIVERSARY, 1943. At APG, the Ordnance School took one special night away from the war to celebrate the 40th anniversary of its founding. (Courtesy U.S. Army.)

SINGING GROUP AT THE ORDNANCE SCHOOL'S 40TH ANNIVERSARY, 1943. The Ordnance School had a lot to sing about, especially with the opening of the new Training School campus at APG in 1940, which was at its peak of training in 1943. (Courtesy U.S. Army.)

FOOD PRESENTATION AT THE ORDNANCE SCHOOL'S 40TH ANNIVERSARY, 1943. From the mess halls of Sandy Hook to the elegant service at its anniversary, the Ordnance School proved that, to paraphrase Napoleon, an army may travel on its stomach, but it won't win a war without ordnance. (Courtesy U.S. Army.)

EDGEWOOD ARSENAL'S OFFICERS' CLUB, MARCH 1925. Photographed on the tennis court are, from left to right, (first row) George A. Sachs, John G. Hartnett, and Roscoe W. Carter; (second row) Harold W. Walker, J. W. Montgomery, and Lester J. Conkling; (third row) Bertyl G. Buckland, Frank C. Whitney, Thomas Dawson, Herbert Hudson, Paul O. Rockwell, and Ralph W. Peake. (Courtesy U.S. Army.)

Six

A LEGACY OF
INNOVATION

SHERIDAN TANK TESTING, 1968. M551, the Sheridan Weapon System, completed testing at Fort Knox, Kentucky. Aspects of battlefield functionality were checked at other test centers, including APG. This final chapter highlights just a few of the changes and challenges that have come since the end of World War II but especially the innovations that benefit everyone. (Courtesy the Historical Society of Harford County.)

ENIAC. This was the mother of all modern computers—the Electronic Numerical Integrater and Computer (ENIAC), the first electronic digital computer. It weighed around 30 tons, used 17,000 vacuum tubes, and was tended by specially trained women who, legend has it, wore roller skates. Lt. Herman Goldstine of the ballistics research lab supported ENIAC's creation (called Project PX) and pushed for funding of the $500,000 project. Dr. John Mauchly and J. Presper Eckert unveiled the machine to the public on Valentine's Day of 1946. Funding further computer production would be a tough sell to a strapped postwar military; the investors turned to the private sector. (Courtesy the Historical Society of Harford County.)

COMPUTERS GET SMALLER, PART ONE. The inventors of ENIAC were allowed to take the specs to IBM in hopes of having the computers built by the public sector. But at IBM, they were told that the company couldn't see a future for a large number of computer sales—maybe 50 at most. Mauchly and Eckert founded their own company called Univac to produce computers and sell them, but they failed. (Courtesy U.S. Army.)

COMPUTERS GET SMALLER, PART TWO. Mauchly and Eckert were just slightly ahead of their time, but their persistence inspired others. In just a few decades, the computing power of ENIAC, the 30-ton beast, would be available in the simplest and cheapest pocket calculators. (Courtesy U.S. Army.)

SHERIDAN TANK TESTING, 1968. Trying to capture over 60 years of change and innovation at APG is daunting, especially since some of beautiful new buildings that house science, health, and technology research, development, and testing cannot be photographed because of security concerns. (Courtesy the Historical Society of Harford County.)

MUNSON TEST TRACK. Much of the work that had been done by scientists and technicians who were part of the military is now done by a small army of private consultants and huge contractors, such as Battelle. But one thing has remained sure—APG is home to innovation. (Courtesy U.S. Army.)

WATER TESTING A TANK. In 1991, Pres. George H. W. Bush committed the United States to destroying all chemical weapons and to renounce the right to chemical weapon retaliation. The U.S. Congress passed legislation requiring the destruction of the entire chemical stockpile—all the bulk containers of chemicals and those chemicals stored in ammunition, most of which is obsolete. (Courtesy U.S. Army.)

VEHICLE TERRAIN TESTING. According to the army, "In February 2006, workers at the Aberdeen Chemical Agent Disposal Facility completed destruction operations by cleaning and decontaminating the last formerly mustard-filled ton container stored at the Edgewood Chemical Activity. Aberdeen is the first site within the continental United States to complete stockpile destruction operations and begin facility closure activities." (Courtesy the Historical Society of Harford County.)

PUTTING A TANK TO THE TEST. "As of January 2007," the army reported, "More than 42 percent of the total U.S. stockpile has been safely destroyed. This is equivalent to 13,231 US tons of chemical agent and nearly 1.8 million munitions." (Courtesy the Historical Society of Harford County.)

SERVICE WITH A SMILE, MAY 13, 1969.
Pfc. Sandy McNamee, a military pay specialist in APG Finance Division, smiles as she adds the finishing touches to a pay voucher. (Courtesy the Historical Society of Harford County.)

COMPUTING PAY, MAY 13, 1969.
Sp4c. Deborah A. Cooper, a military pay specialist, worked with the Finance Division. (Courtesy the Historical Society of Harford County.)

CROWNING OF SPRING QUEEN, 1970. To some folks, 1970 seems like yesterday; to others, it is ancient history. This photograph of the crowning of the spring queen seems to be one to linger on for a moment. Like any ritual, this speaks of cycles, of new years, and of things continuing. Styles change—dresses and hairstyles certainly do—yet no matter where they work or live, couples come together, settle down, and have families, and the cycle begins anew. What better reason to celebrate the crowning of a spring queen in 1970 or today or in 2037? What better reason for being hopeful about the future? (Courtesy the Historical Society of Harford County.)

ABERDEEN HIGH SCHOOL, 1965. The town of Aberdeen grew as Harford County itself began its population explosion in the 1960s, continuing right through today. The new Aberdeen High School with the Math and Science Academy has since opened, while the one in the postcard here has become an educational resource center. (Courtesy Terry Noye.)

THE PATIO DRIVE-IN. At one time, APG was the reason for spikes of growth in local population as folks came seeking jobs or settled down here after their military service, and then things settled back to normal. But Harford County has grown over the past few decades, because it is desirable as a rural getaway from the city and burgeoning counties. It has become a bedroom community, no longer quite so rural. (Courtesy U.S. Army.)

POST EXCHANGE SERVICE STATION. Harford County no longer has an agricultural economy but instead a service economy. Fortunately there are still many rural areas of the county outside the development zones. APG holds the seeds of the technology economy to come. The burger joints and cars of today will be tomorrow's nostalgia. (Courtesy U.S. Army.)

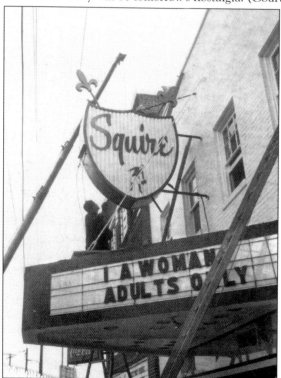

SQUIRE THEATER, ABERDEEN. Times have changed since the New Theater showed classic love stories. The Swedish film *I, a Woman* was first released in 1965. Today the space where the theater was is used as the parking lot for Harford Bank. (Courtesy the Historical Society of Harford County.)

RYAN BUILDING. In 1967, the metal and glass Ordnance Museum building was converted into the new home of the U.S. Army Test and Evaluation Command Headquarters, named the Ryan Building after Brig. Gen. William F. Ryan, the first commander of the U.S. Army Test and Evaluation Command. (Courtesy the Historical Society of Harford County.)

TANK GROUNDS, 1974. The 35-acre field surrounds the Ordnance Museum. The large, gray railway gun in the upper left is the German-nicknamed "Leopold" used against American troops at Anzio in World War II. The outdoor collection includes tanks, guided missiles, rockets, and other types of mobile equipment. (Courtesy the Historical Society of Harford County.)

NEW MUSEUM TAKES SHAPE. The hallmark of the new museum is the 43,600-pound T-12 general-purpose bomb cleverly set up to appear as it might at impact, with its nose hitting the target. (Courtesy the Historical Society of Harford County.)

MUSEUM OPENS. The Ordnance Museum's ribbon cutting was held on May 18, 1973. In the first eight months following the museum's reopening, over 80,000 visitors saw the ordnance materiel displays. (Courtesy the Historical Society of Harford County.)

BATTLE OF THE BULGE DIORAMA, 1974. Based on real-life stories from battle participants, this life-size scene depicts an American outpost being overrun by Germans. Exhibit specialist Clarence Lewis positions a rifle as this motorcyclist would have carried it. (Courtesy the Historical Society of Harford County.)

THE ATOMIC CANNON. This U.S. 280-mm M65 gun is one of the massive weapons on display on the grounds of APG. (Courtesy the Historical Society of Harford County.)

GENERAL PERSHING'S LOCOMOBILE. The 1916 Dodge touring car was completely rebuilt. It had been driven by Sgt. Eddie Rickenbacker (the top American ace in World War I and Medal of Honor recipient) for Gen. John J. "Blackjack" Pershing during World War I. Gen. George S. Patton was a passenger as well. On display at the museum, the car serves as a direct link to APG's earliest days of service. (Courtesy the Historical Society of Harford County.)

PARTING SHOT. Aberdeen Proving Ground began with the relocation of the Ordnance Command from the Sandy Hook Proving Ground at Fort Hancock, New Jersey, where this fellow had his photograph taken 100 years ago; now APG is to be enriched by the addition of the Communications-Electronics Command from Fort Monmouth, New Jersey. As the Ordnance Command moves away from APG to Fort Lee, Virginia, and personnel from Fort Monmouth move in, great changes are underway. Undoubtedly APG will continue its tradition of leadership in the development and perfection of new technologies. And, just as surely, the army will continue to find support in the citizens of Harford County. Back in 1919, following the war and the shutting down of the production plants at Edgewood, one veteran wrote that the public recognition received by his fellow veterans from Edgewood Arsenal and APG "is so wholly inadequate, considering the nature of the work they have accomplished and the high percentage of the casualties they have endured." This book is meant to help keep their sacrifices in memory. (Courtesy U.S. Army.)

ACROSS AMERICA, PEOPLE ARE DISCOVERING SOMETHING WONDERFUL. *THEIR HERITAGE.*

Arcadia Publishing is the leading local history publisher in the United States. With more than 3,000 titles in print and hundreds of new titles released every year, Arcadia has extensive specialized experience chronicling the history of communities and celebrating America's hidden stories, bringing to life the people, places, and events from the past. To discover the history of other communities across the nation, please visit:

www.arcadiapublishing.com

Customized search tools allow you to find regional history books about the town where you grew up, the cities where your friends and family live, the town where your parents met, or even that retirement spot you've been dreaming about.